New Jersey

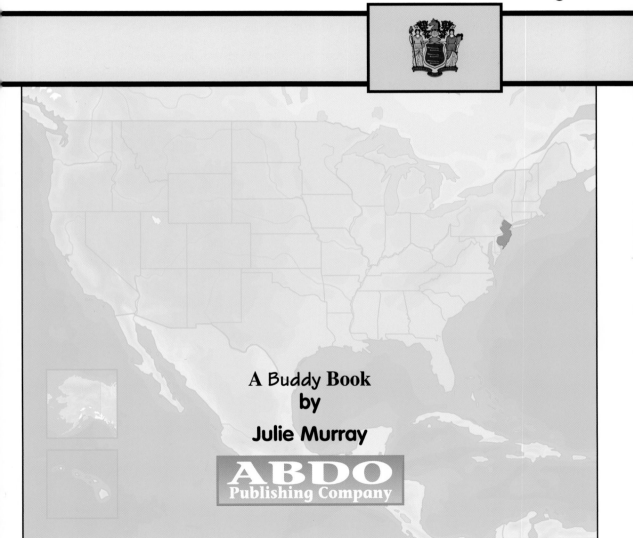

A Buddy Book
by
Julie Murray

ABDO
Publishing Company

VISIT US AT
www.abdopub.com

Published by ABDO Publishing Company, 4940 Viking Drive, Edina, Minnesota 55435.

Copyright © 2006 by Abdo Consulting Group, Inc. International copyrights reserved in all countries. No part of this book may be reproduced in any form without written permission from the publisher. Buddy Books™ is a trademark and logo of ABDO Publishing Company.

Printed in the United States.

Edited by: Sarah Tieck
Contributing Editor: Michael P. Goecke
Graphic Design: Deb Coldiron, Maria Hosley
Image Research: Sarah Tieck
Photographs: Clipart.com, Creatas, Getty Images, Image100, Library of Congress, One Mile Up, PhotoDisc

Library of Congress Cataloging-in-Publication Data

Murray, Julie, 1969-
    New Jersey / Julie Murray.
        p. cm. — (The United States)
    Includes bibliographical references and index.
    ISBN 1-59197-689-8
        1. New Jersey—Juvenile literature. I. Title.

F134.3.M87 2005
974.9—dc22

2005046955

Table Of Contents

A Snapshot Of New Jersey

When people think of New Jersey, they think of an industrial state. But, this state also has beaches, farmland, mountains, waterfalls, and lakes.

A sandy beach in New Jersey.

There are 50 states in the United States. Every state is different. Every state has an official nickname. New Jersey is known as the "Garden State." This is because of its agriculture.

Many people live in New Jersey.

New Jersey became the third state on December 18, 1787. It is the fifth-smallest state in United States. New Jersey has only 7,790 square miles (20,176 sq km) of land. It is home to 8,414,350 people.

Where Is New Jersey?

There are four parts of the United States. Each part is called a region. Each region is in a different area of the country. The United States Census Bureau says the four regions are the Northeast, the South, the Midwest, and the West.

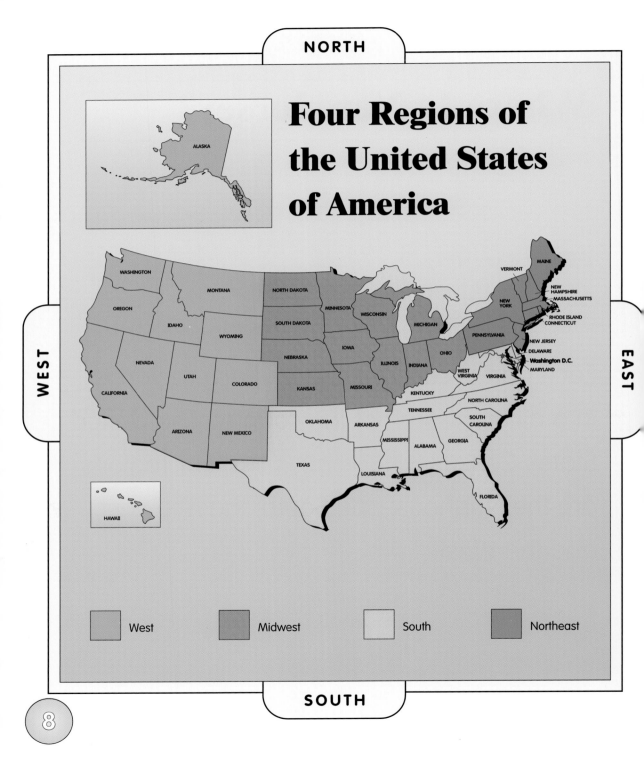

Four Regions of the United States of America

ALASKA

WASHINGTON

OREGON

IDAHO

MONTANA

WYOMING

NEVADA

UTAH

CALIFORNIA

ARIZONA

NEW MEXICO

COLORADO

NORTH DAKOTA

SOUTH DAKOTA

NEBRASKA

KANSAS

OKLAHOMA

TEXAS

MINNESOTA

IOWA

MISSOURI

ARKANSAS

LOUISIANA

WISCONSIN

ILLINOIS

MICHIGAN

INDIANA

OHIO

KENTUCKY

TENNESSEE

MISSISSIPPI

ALABAMA

GEORGIA

WEST VIRGINIA

VIRGINIA

NORTH CAROLINA

SOUTH CAROLINA

FLORIDA

VERMONT

MAINE

NEW YORK

NEW HAMPSHIRE

MASSACHUSETTS

RHODE ISLAND

CONNECTICUT

PENNSYLVANIA

NEW JERSEY

DELAWARE

Washington D.C.

MARYLAND

HAWAII

West

Midwest

South

Northeast

New Jersey is located in the Northeast region of the United States. New Jersey has four seasons. The seasons are spring, summer, fall, and winter. New Jersey's temperatures are mild.

Sometimes New Jersey gets snow in the winter months.

New Jersey is surrounded by water and shares its borders with three states. Delaware and Pennsylvania are to the west, across the Delaware River. New York is to the north. The Hudson River forms the northeast border of the state. The Atlantic Ocean is east. Delaware Bay is south.

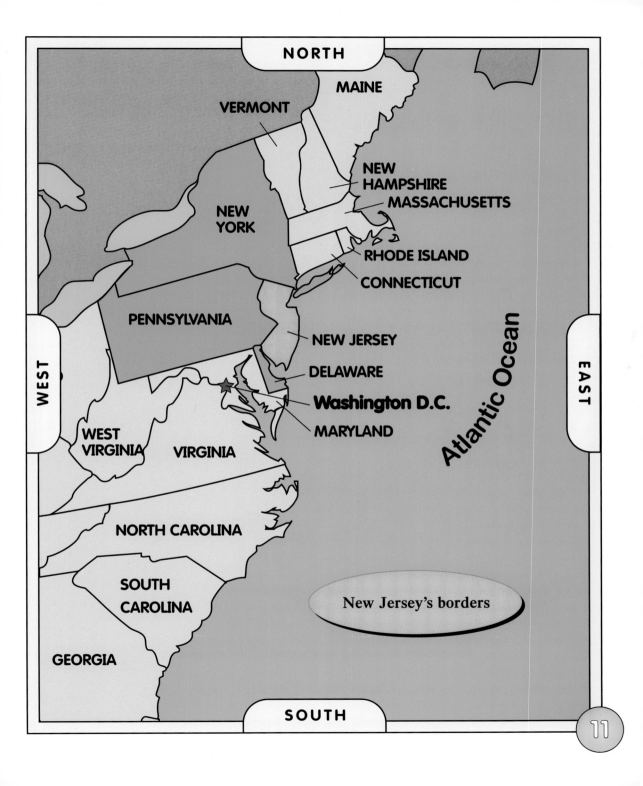

NORTH

MAINE

VERMONT

NEW
HAMPSHIRE

MASSACHUSETTS

NEW
YORK

RHODE ISLAND

CONNECTICUT

PENNSYLVANIA

NEW JERSEY

DELAWARE

WEST

EAST

Washington D.C.

Atlantic Ocean

MARYLAND

WEST
VIRGINIA

VIRGINIA

NORTH CAROLINA

SOUTH
CAROLINA

New Jersey's borders

GEORGIA

SOUTH

New Jersey

State abbreviation: NJ

State nickname: Garden State

State capital: Trenton

State motto: Liberty and Prosperity

Statehood: December 18, 1787, third state

Population: 8,414,350, ranks ninth

Land area: 7,790 square miles (20,176 sq km), ranks 46th

State flag:
Adopted in 1896

State tree: Red oak

State song: "I'm From New Jersey"

State government: Three branches: legislative, executive, and judicial

State flower: Violet

Average July temperature: 75°F (24°C)

Average January temperature: 31°F (-1°C)

State animal: Horse

State bird: Eastern goldfinch

Cities And The Capital

Newark is the largest city in New Jersey. It is located in the northeast part of the state. Newark is home to many businesses. It is the third-largest insurance center in the United States. Prudential Insurance has its headquarters in Newark.

The airport in Newark.

Trenton became New Jersey's state capital in 1790. It is located along the Delaware River in western New Jersey. Trenton is most famous for the 1776 Battle of Trenton during the American Revolutionary War. General George Washington and his soldiers defeated the Hessian soldiers there.

Famous Citizens

Judy Blume (1938–)

Judy Blume was born in Elizabeth. She is an award-winning author. She writes books for children and adults. Some of her books include

Judy Blume

Superfudge, Otherwise Known as Sheila the Great, Tales of a Fourth Grade Nothing, and *Are You There God? It's Me, Margaret*

Famous Citizens

Grover Cleveland (1837–1908)

Grover Cleveland was born in Caldwell. He is the only United States president to be elected to two nonconsecutive terms. He served as the 22nd president from 1885 to 1889. He was elected again as the 24th president and served from 1893 to 1897.

Grover Cleveland

Washington Crossing

The colonists fought for independence from Great Britain in the American Revolutionary War. This war was from 1775 to 1783.

In November 1776, the British took control of New Jersey. The British hired German soldiers to help them fight. The German soldiers were called Hessians.

George Washington

On Christmas night in 1776, General George Washington and his army crossed the Delaware River to New Jersey. The crossing was dangerous. The weather was cold and windy. Washington's soldiers had to paddle through icy water.

Once across, they defeated the Hessian troops and won the Battle of Trenton.

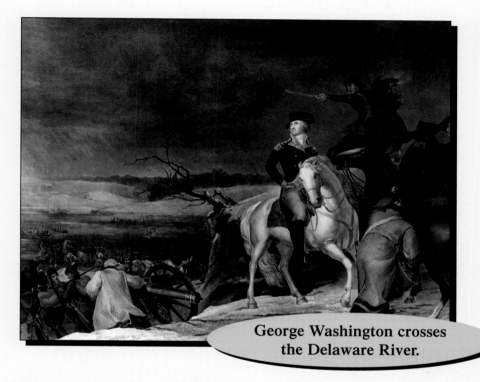

George Washington crosses the Delaware River.

Today, Washington Crossing State Park honors the site where Washington and his army came ashore in 1776. Every Christmas there is a reenactment of the historic crossing.

The Jersey Shore

The Jersey Shore is a popular destination for residents and visitors. The coast along the Atlantic Ocean is about 130 miles (200 km). It runs from Sandy Hook Bay down to Cape May. Tourists can visit beaches, amusement parks, zoos, historical lighthouses, and museums.

Atlantic City is the largest city along the Jersey Shore. It attracts millions of people each year. It is famous for its boardwalk and casinos. Atlantic City hosted the first Miss America Pageant in 1921.

A view of Atlantic City.

Delaware Water Gap

The Delaware Water Gap National Recreation Area is 70,000 acres (28,328 ha) of land along the Delaware River. The park is in both New Jersey and Pennsylvania. The Delaware River provides drinking water to millions of people in neighboring areas.

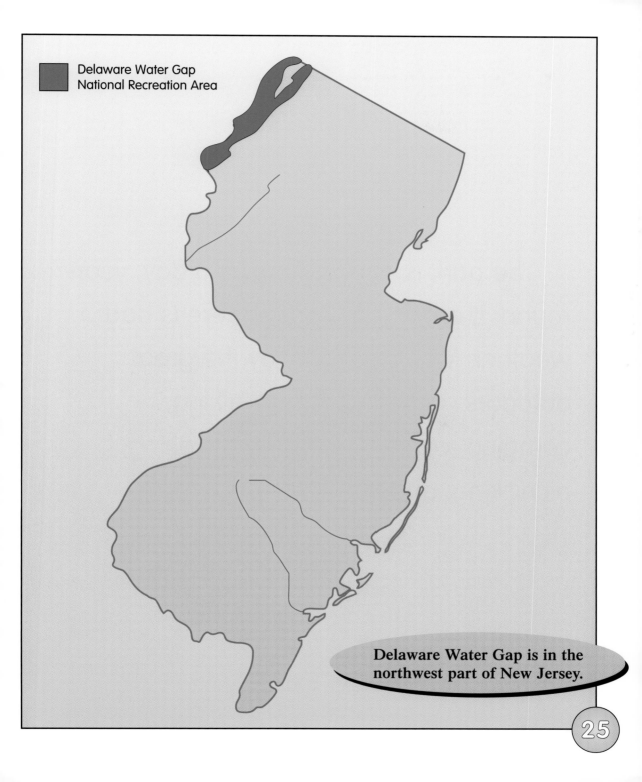

Delaware Water Gap
National Recreation Area

Delaware Water Gap is in the
northwest part of New Jersey.

The park is open 24 hours a day, year-round. It only closes when there is bad weather. Visitors can enjoy the great outdoors. Activities include biking, camping, canoeing, hiking, kayaking, picnicking, and river rafting.

People visit the Delaware Water
Gap in every season

New Jersey

1524: Giovanni da Verrazzano explores New Jersey's coast.

1609: Henry Hudson explores Sandy Hook Bay.

1660: Bergen is the first town in New Jersey. It will later be called Jersey City.

1664: The British take control of New Jersey.

1766: Rutgers University is founded in New Jersey.

1776: George Washington and his army cross the Delaware River and win the Battle of Trenton.

1787: New Jersey is the third state to ratify the United States Constitution.

1789: New Jersey is the first state to sign the Bill of Rights.

1804: Alexander Hamilton and Aaron Burr have their famous duel in Weehawken.

1858: First nearly complete dinosaur fossil is found in Haddonfield.

1879: Thomas Edison invents an incandescent lamp.

1882: The first amusement pier is built in Atlantic City.

1921: The first Miss America Pageant is held in Atlantic City.

1933: The first drive-in movie theater in the United States opens in Camden.

1952: The New Jersey Turnpike opens.

1994: Christine Todd Whitman becomes the first female governor of New Jersey.

2005: Newark celebrates its 340th birthday.

Atlantic City

Cities In New Jersey

Paterson

Caldwell

Newark • • Weehawken
Elizabeth • • Jersey City

New Brunswick

Trenton

Asbury Park

Camden •
• Haddonfield

Atlantic City

Important Words

American Revolutionary War Americans fought for freedom from Great Britain in this famous war.

capital a city where government leaders meet.

casino a place where adults gamble.

colonist a person who lives in a settlement called a colony.

headquarters a center of operation.

Hessian a soldier from Germany employed by the British to fight in the American Revolutionary War.

industrial production and sale of goods and services.

nickname a name that describes something special about a person or a place.

nonconsecutive not following in sequence or order.

Web Sites

To learn more about New Jersey, visit ABDO Publishing Company on the World Wide Web. Web site links about New Jersey are featured on our Book Links page. These links are routinely monitored and updated to provide the most current information available.

www.abdopub.com

Index